Born
THIS HAPPY
MORNING

Born THIS HAPPY MORNING

JOHN BYTHEWAY

DESERET
BOOK

SALT LAKE CITY, UTAH

Interior background image Myimagine/Shutterstock.com

Library of Congress Cataloging-in-Publication Data

Names: Bytheway, John, 1962– author.
Title: Born this happy morning / John Bytheway.
Description: Salt Lake City, Utah : Deseret Book, [2020] | Includes bibliographical references. | Summary: "Best-selling Latter-day Saint author John Bytheway discusses the kinds of joy we can receive while celebrating the birth of Jesus Christ at Christmastime"—Provided by publisher.
Identifiers: LCCN 2020018712 | ISBN 9781629728056 (trade paperback)
Subjects: LCSH: Jesus Christ—Nativity. | The Church of Jesus Christ of Latter-day Saints—Doctrines. | Generosity—Religious aspects—Christianity. | Gifts—Religious aspects—Christianity. | Christmas.
Classification: LCC BV4647.G45 B97 2020 | DDC 263/.915—dc23
LC record available at https://lccn.loc.gov/2020018712

Printed in the United States of America
PubLitho, Draper, UT

10   9   8   7   6   5   4   3   2   1

Note: These chapters were composed under the influence of a fresh balsam fir–scented candle, chestnuts roasting on a screen saver, and yuletide carols being sung by the Tabernacle Choir. (Mama was in her kerchief, and I in my cap.)

For a more holly-jolly experience, readers are invited to reproduce similar sights, smells, and sounds while perusing these chapters.

And finally, no reindeer were harmed during this book's production; however, several halls were decked.

CONTENTS

INTRODUCTION

$\mathcal{A}$s a little boy, I began thinking about Christmas each year sometime in the fall, about the time the weather began to turn cold. I just couldn't wait. I counted the months and days and eagerly waited for the "Sears Wishbook" to arrive so I could gaze for hours at every single page in the toy section. The day that school got out for Christmas vacation, my siblings and I would run home giggling in delight. We'd spend evenings sitting beneath the tree, watching the lights twinkle and create patterns on the ceiling while carols played in the background.

Now, some decades later, as an adult, a provider, and a father, I don't have much time to think about

Christmas until the Thanksgiving leftovers are gone. Amidst the adult concerns, budgets, and overall stress, I find myself trying to recapture the magic of Christmas as I remember it from my days as a child. I miss it. Almost every Christmas season, I say to my wife, Kim, "I just haven't quite caught the spirit."

Eventually, though, that Christmas feeling comes— often later than I would like, but it comes. It comes when I hear the Tabernacle Choir sing sacred carols, when I get home from work and smell the aroma of Christmas candles in the house, or when I watch Ebenezer Scrooge being born again on the TV. It comes when I watch my children shop for each other and find the perfect gift.

The conclusion I've come to is that Christmas is a *feeling*. Above all else, what we want, what we hope for during the season, what we are craving, is a feeling. Thankfully, the feeling of Christmas has been captured in Christmas carols, Christmas stories, and Christmas movies. I assume people read Christmas books for the same reason. They want to feel something! They want to feel that spirit of Christmas again.

President Thomas S. Monson said:

The spirit of Christmas illuminates the picture window of the soul. . . . To catch the real meaning of the spirit of Christmas, we need only drop the last syllable, and it becomes the Spirit of Christ.

My friend and colleague Hank Smith pointed out a beautiful insight found in our Bible Dictionary under the heading "Miracles." It describes miracles as "the natural results of the Messiah's presence among men." Hank observed that as the holiday season approaches, the name of Christ, the first syllable of the word *Christmas*, appears on cards, banners, letters, even advertisements. Notice the natural result! People are nicer, they smile more, and a spirit of giving, excitement, and anticipation lies over the world like a warm, comforting blanket during a chilly season. It is truly miraculous.

The third verse of "Oh, Come, All Ye Faithful" begins, "Yea, Lord, we greet thee, born this happy morning." Yes, what a happy morning! Jesus came. After thousands of years of prophecies promising that He would come, He came, and we are saved, we are rescued, we are redeemed.

That first Christmas Eve—that late night and early morning—is an important focal point in Christian history because of what the babe in the manger became and what He accomplished. As the hymn "O Little Town of Bethlehem" so accurately states, "The hopes and fears of all the years are met in thee tonight."

We receive priceless gifts from the Savior throughout our lives, but at Christmas we remember particularly that happy night and that happy morning. Because of that one special eve in history, and because of the impact of Jesus Christ on the world, mankind pushed the reset button on the calendar and started counting the years from that night forward. As a child, when I saw the year written down, I knew that "BC" meant "before Christ," but I erroneously thought "AD" meant "after death." I learned later that "AD" stood for the Latin phrase *Anno Domini*, or "the year of our Lord." It hadn't occurred to me before, but every time we are mentioning what year it is, we are remembering Christmas. We are saying, "It's been this many years since Christ was born."

How else can we remember Christmas? How else can we capture that Christmas feeling, that mixture of joy, hope, and anticipation that seems to be in the air on Christmas Eve? Can we make those wonderful feelings stay for a while? Is it possible to feel Christmas all year round? I sure hope so! Let's give it a try.

"Through all of our various Christmas traditions, I hope that we are focused first upon the Lord Jesus Christ. Wise men still adore Him."

—*Russell M. Nelson*

CHAPTER ONE

THE THREE LEVELS OF CHRISTMAS JOY

*Y*ears ago, I came across an insightful editorial originally published in the *Church News* called "The Three Levels of Christmas." The author, William B. Smart, former editor and general manager of the *Deseret News*, explained that the Christmas holiday can be experienced on three levels.

The Fun of Level One

The first level, Brother Smart explained, is the "Santa Claus" level. "It's the level at which we eat too much and spend too much and do too much—and enjoy every minute of it. We love the Santa Claus level of Christmas."

The Jack and Diane Bytheway children, basking in the warm glow of a level-one Christmas. (I'm in the lower left corner.)

I agree! I enjoy this level too! The first level includes jolly old Saint Nick, eight tiny reindeer, decorated Christmas trees, twinkling lights, stockings hung by the chimney with care, and a spirit of great anticipation. Some of my most cherished childhood memories involve enjoying Christmas with my brothers and sisters.

It's probably fair to say that the world is most focused on the Santa Claus level of Christmas (which most of us love). Sadly, they're too often stuck there. It's a commercial windfall, and the stores are packed with shoppers. The day after Thanksgiving has been called "Black Friday" because that is when many retailers generate enough sales to finally get out of the red (debt), and into the black (profits). More recently, we've added "Cyber Monday," with its millions of online purchases, signaling that the Santa Claus level is fully underway. (And if you order today, free shipping!)

The Joy of Level Two

Brother Smart called the second level the "Silent Night" level. On this level, we are more focused on the "reason for the season," the birth of Jesus Christ. This level is captured in the Nativity scenes we display in our homes depicting the Holy Family, the shepherds, the star, and the wise men bringing gifts from the East.

Level two is not just about Christmas Day; it encompasses the entire holiday season, and the holiday season is often associated with the feeling of joy. The word *joy* appears on decorations, Christmas cards, and ornaments. It is sprinkled throughout the lyrics of our favorite carols, most notably in one of our hymns, "Joy to the World." In the scriptures, an angel proclaimed that joy was coming when he made the announcement of the birth of Christ to the shepherds:

And the angel said unto them, Fear not: for, behold, I bring you good tidings of great joy, which shall be to all people. For unto you is born this day in the city of David a Saviour, which is Christ the Lord. (Luke 2:10–11)

As we've shared the Luke 2 account with our family, my children have wondered what is meant by the word *tidings*. In Webster's 1828 dictionary, *tidings* are defined as "news; advice; information; intelligence; account of what has taken place, and was not known before." *Tidings* is just another way of saying "news." In these latter days, *news* is often a depressing word. We say, "No news is good news." We might even avoid watching the news because it's too depressing. In our day-to-day living, I've discovered I often call my wife with the less-than-joyous greeting, "Do you want to hear the good news or the bad news?"

By contrast, we don't use the word *tidings* very often today. CNN is not CTN, the Cable Tidings Network; we don't log onto FoxTidings.com to check the headlines. I'm glad that *tidings* has remained such a positive word. Scripturally speaking, *tidings* has become almost exclusively a good-news word, often a

Christmas word, and spreading Christmas tidings is part of an angelic assignment.

Can you imagine the calling given to one special angel to visit earth and happily announce, "I bring you good tidings of great joy"? That's got to be one of the best assignments any angel could receive. Some angels come down to earth to scold, but this one came to celebrate, to encourage, to bring the greatest news ever. He came to bring joy!

The shepherds might have wondered about the reason for the promised joy, so the angel continued, "For unto you is born this day in the city of David a Saviour, which is Christ the Lord" (Luke 2:11). The angel directly connected the feeling of joy with the birth of the Savior, and indeed, He is the source of true joy. And then, if you can imagine the spectacle, as soon as the angel concluded his happy message, "Suddenly there was with the angel a multitude of the heavenly host praising God, and saying, Glory to God in the highest, and on earth peace, good will toward men" (Luke 2:13–14). An angelic announcement followed by a backup choir of the heavenly host—that's got to be a really great day for an angel.

In the Book of Mormon, it was an angel who helped King Benjamin write his famous address—perhaps the same angel who visited the shepherds in Bethlehem, because he used the same phrase! King Benjamin reported the words of the heavenly messenger:

> *And he said unto me: Awake, and hear the words which I shall tell thee; for behold, I am come to declare unto you the* glad tidings of great joy. . . . *For behold, the time cometh, and is not far distant, that with power, the Lord Omnipotent who reigneth, who was, and is from all eternity to all eternity, shall come down from heaven among the children of men. (Mosiah 3:3, 5; emphasis added)*

Several decades later, Alma told his struggling son Corianton about the "coming of Christ" (which began at Christmas) and declared, "He cometh to declare glad tidings of salvation unto his people" (Alma 39:15).

As the birth of Christ drew closer, Samuel the Lamanite prophesied of signs and wonders of light in the New World related to the birth of the Savior. Notice the phrases used in the book of Helaman to describe the years leading up to that first Christmas:

And angels did appear unto men, wise men, and did declare unto them glad tidings of great joy; thus in this year the scriptures began to be fulfilled. (Helaman 16:14)

It's pretty hard to miss the Christmas phrases in that short verse: "wise men," "glad tidings," "great joy"! All have become like code words for Christmas. In the very next chapter, Mormon reports:

And thus the ninety and second year did pass away, bringing glad tidings unto the people because of the signs which did come to pass, according to the words of the prophecy of all the holy prophets. (3 Nephi 1:26)

There are those glad tidings again!

We know, from one of the most profound statements of Father Lehi, that "Adam fell that men might be; and men are, that they might have joy" (2 Nephi 2:25).

Joy is my favorite word in that verse—but the most intriguing word in Lehi's statement could be the word *might*. In other words, you might have joy, but then again, you might not. The possibility of joy in this life is mentioned, but it's not guaranteed. We'll have plenty of ups and downs. Similarly, we are reminded of the words in the Declaration of Independence concerning the rights to "Life, Liberty and the pursuit of Happiness." An absolute guarantee of happiness is not offered, but the right to pursue it is.

Enoch knew that not every day of mortality is joyful. In a verse that sounds very similar to Lehi's, Enoch taught, "Because that Adam fell, we are; and by his fall came death; and we are made partakers of misery and woe" (Moses 6:48).

In this life, we are here that we might have joy. On other days, we are made partakers of "misery and woe." Sometimes we have 2 Nephi 2:25 days, and sometimes we have Moses 6:48 days. But without the misery and woe days, we might not appreciate the days of joy! That's one of the lessons and one of the fruits of "opposition in all things" (2 Nephi 2:11).

So here's the question: will the day ever come when we can be full of joy, continuous joy, an endless Christmas? The scriptures answer yes—though not in this world, and not in what this world has to offer. But joy is abundantly available in Christ: "Wherefore, fear not even unto death; for in this world your joy is not full, but in me your joy is full" (D&C 101:36).

There is the key, the key to lasting joy. Real joy is in Christ. As President Russell M. Nelson observed:

> *The joy we feel has little to do with the circumstances of our lives and everything to do with the focus of our lives. When the focus of our lives is on God's plan of salvation . . . and Jesus Christ and His gospel, we can feel joy regardless of what is happening—or not happening—in our lives. Joy comes from and because of Him. He is the source of all joy.*

Which leads us beyond level two into level three:

The Power of Level Three

Brother Smart observed that even with all that level one and level two of Christmas have to offer, something is still missing: "The angels and the star, and the shepherd, even the silent, sacred mystery of the holy night itself, can't long satisfy humanity's basic need. The man who keeps Christ in the manger will, in the end, be disappointed and empty."

I appreciate that phrase, *the man who keeps Christ in the manger*, because it often seems as if that is exactly what the worldly are trying to do with this holiday— either stay focused on Santa Claus only, or, if they acknowledge Christ at all, keep Him in the manger. Although the baby Jesus is mentioned at Christmas, many have pushed back against this level by replacing "Merry Christmas" with "Happy Holidays" and "Christmas programs" with "winter festivals."

"For Christmas to last all year long," Brother Smart continued, "for it to grow in beauty and meaning and purpose, for it to have the power to change lives, we must celebrate it at the third level, that of the adult Christ. It is at this level—not as an infant—that our Savior brings his gifts of lasting joy, lasting peace, lasting hope."

We all know that the first verses of Luke 2 tell the story of Jesus's birth; but the chapter continues with these lines: "The child grew, and waxed strong in spirit, filled with wisdom: and the grace of God was upon him" (Luke 2:40). Then the child became a man, as Luke reports, "and Jesus increased in wisdom and stature, and in favour with God and man" (Luke 2:52). The adult Christ, and all that He accomplished in our behalf as an adult, is exactly why we refer to His Nativity as a "happy morning."

Level two celebrates the baby Jesus, but level three

is about Christ the *Lord*, the newborn *King*. The world finds it relatively easy to acknowledge the birth of a baby who can't really say anything. But Jesus grew, and He learned. The adult Christ loved and served, but He also repeated lines from the Old Testament, which said things like "thou shalt not." Some people were downright uncomfortable with the adult Jesus. He told the rich young man to sell all that he had, give it to the poor, and follow Him (see Matthew 19:16–21). The rich young man, who went away sorrowing, might have preferred the baby Jesus, who didn't walk around exhorting, expounding, and repeating commandments.

But it was also the adult Jesus who performed the Atonement and saved all of us from sin and death. It was the adult Jesus whose body was missing when the women went to the tomb. Without Easter, of course, there would be no reason to celebrate Christmas! The greatest triumph of the adult Jesus was the empty tomb—and that's level three. The happy morning of His birth was followed some thirty-three years later by Resurrection morning, the greatest miracle and greatest triumph of the adult Christ.

Now, I am going to make a confession: I love

Christmas at all three levels. As a child, I wasn't thinking to myself, "This is all too commercial; let's just forget all the gift giving and sing hymns." Nope, I still love level one. I love "Jingle Bells," and Santa Claus, and blinking lights, and I thoroughly enjoy level one of Christmas every season.

I also love level two, the Silent Night level. I love listening to the sacred carols about Bethlehem, Mary, Joseph, the shepherds, and all those who surround them asking, "Do You Hear What I Hear?" and (perhaps the most important question of all), "What Child Is This?" But Brother Smart is absolutely right—Christmas wouldn't be celebrated at all without level three, the adult Christ.

Christ the Lord is the source of all joy and all good tidings. When it comes to Christmas, tidings are the good news, and joy is the feeling the tidings bring. We can experience the joy of Christmas by sharing it on its many levels with others—neighbors, friends, family members, and even brothers and sisters we've never met but whom the Lord has placed in our path.

"Love is one of the chief characteristics of Deity, and ought to be manifested by those who aspire to be the sons of God. A man filled with the love of God, is not content with blessing his family alone, but ranges through the whole world, anxious to bless the whole human race."

—*Joseph Smith*

CHAPTER TWO

THE JOY OF GIVING ANONYMOUSLY

*J*have a list of "must-do" items each Christmas. I suspect you do too. My list includes sights, sounds, and, of course, tastes. One item on my list, a traditional ritual from as far back as I can remember, is to watch the movie *A Christmas Carol*.

Charles Dickens's story of Ebenezer Scrooge has become such a classic that a recent movie about Dickens and his inspiration in writing the tale is actually titled *The Man Who Invented Christmas*. Well, that title is a little too strong: Dickens didn't invent Christmas, but his tale of Scrooge's transformation has certainly become a part of the celebration for many of us.

A quick search on ChurchofJesusChrist.org reveals

that Dickens's story of Scrooge is so widely loved and appreciated that it has been frequently mentioned in general conference talks. For example, Elder L. Whitney Clayton observed:

Every year, as we watch Ebenezer Scrooge undertake his miraculous transformation from a heartless hermit into a happy neighbor filled with Christmas joy, we feel the tug to let go of the Scrooge within us. We feel prompted to do a little better to follow the Savior's example of charity to all.

I'm not a movie critic, but of all the different movie versions of the story of Scrooge, featuring such notable actors as George C. Scott, Patrick Stewart, the Muppets, and Jim Carrey, my choice is and will probably always be the 1951 version starring Alastair Sim. For me, this particular Scrooge's transition from the spirit of miserly bitterness to the spirit of Christmas is the most beautiful, believable, and tear inducing.

I suspect most of us are familiar with the story, and yet we watch it again every year. When it comes to Christmas, we don't mind reruns! In that spirit, would you permit me to rewind some of my favorite parts of the story and share them with you?

As Scrooge awakens from his visits of the Ghosts of Christmas Past, Present, and Future and gleefully realizes he is still alive, he is filled with joy and a resolve to change the man he used to be into the man he could be. In his excitement, he dances around the room, he rejoices in everything he sees, and he feels as "light as a feather, as merry as a schoolboy, and as giddy as a drunken man."

One of his first actions is to stick his head out the window, perhaps to hear the Christmas bells chime and breathe in the atmosphere of Christmas morning. Seeing a little boy run down the street, he stops him and asks him to go get the butcher and bring him back, along with the prize turkey. As the arrangements are made, he mutters to himself about the young man: "What an intelligent boy, a remarkable boy, a delightful boy, an enchanting boy!" This man, you'll remember, is the same man who rudely ordered carolers away the night before with an irritated "Be off with you!"

Is he going to buy the turkey for himself? No. He cannot wait to send it to the home of his clerk,

Bob Cratchit. As he scribbles the address on a label, he giggles with excitement as he says to himself, "He'll never dream where it came from!" This will be a gift from an unknown giver. There will be no "To: Bob, From: Ebenezer" on the tag. Nope. He wants it to arrive anonymously, which it does, filling the stunned Cratchit family with joy and wonder. Only an inspired Tiny Tim suspects that it might have come from Scrooge.

The next morning, when Bob Cratchit arrives a few minutes late for his bookkeeping duties, Ebenezer Scrooge leads him to believe he might be fired. After a few tense moments, Scrooge calls Bob to his desk and declares, "I'm not going to stand for this sort of thing any longer—which leaves me no alternative . . . but to raise your salary!" Bob stands in stunned silence, and then Scrooge's entire countenance transforms.

An immobile Bob Cratchit stands transfixed as Scrooge begins to laugh with joy. Finally, he explains, "Bob, I haven't lost my senses, I've come to them. I want to help you raise that little family of yours, if you'll let me. We'll discuss it later over a bowl of hot punch. But right now, you go out and buy a new coal scuttle, and you do that before you dot another 'i,' Bob Cratchit!"

As Cratchit scurries out the door, Scrooge relishes the moment, then mumbles to himself, "I don't deserve to be so happy," as he writes something down. But the joy returns, and he laughs again as he throws his quill pen in the air and exclaims, "But I can't help it—I just can't help it!" I laugh right along with Scrooge every Christmas as I watch.

Now, here's my reason for reliving with you this part of the story. I want us to consider—exactly what was it that overcame Scrooge? Why did he suddenly feel like doing such a wonderful thing? And why did he want to do it anonymously? What Dickens captured in this beautiful story, and what talented actors and moviemakers have also restored for us, is the joy that comes when one is given a merciful chance for a new start, a clean slate, something akin to the joy of being born again. Scrooge was overcome with charity, the pure love of Christ; his joy and gratitude were full to overflowing, and he had to send those feelings somewhere.

And he did. On that Christmas morning, Scrooge

gave his loyal housekeeper a substantial raise. Next, he sent a prize turkey to the Cratchit family anonymously. Also, he found the men who were trying to raise a fund for the poor, whom he had coldly rejected the day before, and whispered in their ears the jaw-dropping amount he wished to contribute, adding, "a great many back payments are included in it, I assure you."

Scrooge gave openly to his housekeeper and the two men seeking meat and drink for the poor, but he also gave anonymously, which is one of the greatest of all Christmas joys.

Secret Acts Rewarded Openly

Jesus spent a good deal of time in the Sermon on the Mount condemning those who did good things for less than the best reasons. Some "sound a trumpet" before they give alms, he explained, that they may have the glory of men. Some love to pray standing in the street corners, to be seen of men. Others disfigure their faces and create a sad countenance to make it appear they are fasting. Of all these groups, Jesus says, "They have their reward" (Matthew 6:2, 5, 16).

Jesus teaches us a better, holier way to serve: "Let

not thy left hand know what thy right hand doeth" (Matthew 6:3). In other words, give joyfully, without desire for recognition of men. Serve so that no one else will know, a type of service that brings its own unique kind of joy. Jesus assures us that although no one on earth may know, someone in heaven will, and He repeats this beautiful promise three times: "Thy Father which seeth in secret himself shall reward thee openly" (Matthew 6:4; see also vv. 6, 18).

Many of us have been recipients of anonymous gifts, which is incredibly humbling. In my family, we have people we sincerely desire to thank, but we don't even know who they are. Recently, our bishop called my wife and me into his office and informed us that a ward member who wished to remain anonymous had made a substantial donation towards our daughter's mission to France.

This generous and anonymous gift had an impact that went way beyond our finances and lasted way beyond our daughter's missionary service. Ever since that day, we look at everyone in our ward a little differently. What a gift! We want to treat each person with a little more kindness and charity, knowing he or she may be the one who helped us. We thank our Heavenly Father for our ward family and pray that whoever they are, wherever they are, the Lord will "reward them openly."

Joseph, Son of Heli

There are a lot of different Josephs in the scriptures whom we respect and honor: Joseph of Egypt, who became Pharaoh's right-hand man; Joseph, son of Lehi, who was born in the wilderness; Joseph of Arimathea, who provided a tomb for Jesus's body; and, of course, Joseph Smith in the latter days. Each Christmas, as we gaze upon our little Nativity scenes, we see standing beside Mary another Joseph—one about whom we know very little.

His genealogy, showing that he was from the lineage of David, appears in the first chapter of Matthew, but we don't know much else. The Bible Dictionary gives us only one paragraph about him, concluding with this line: "It is probable that Joseph died before the Crucifixion (and probably before our Lord's baptism), as otherwise Mary would hardly have been committed by our Lord to the keeping of John (John 19:26–27)."

Obviously, Joseph must have been a righteous man,

chosen long before his mortal life to be espoused to Mary. The angel of the Lord who appeared to him in a dream called him "thou son of David," acknowledging his chosen lineage (Matthew 1:20). Perhaps we could say that Joseph was one of those who served "behind the scenes" in many ways, since we know so little about his life. Elder Jeffrey R. Holland, while outlining different ways we could remember the Savior while partaking of the sacrament, offered this tribute to Joseph:

> *We could remember [Jesus's] magnificent but virtually unknown foster father, a humble carpenter by trade who taught us, among other things, that quiet, plain, unpretentious people have moved this majestic work forward from the very beginning, and still do so today. If you are serving almost anonymously, please know that so, too, did one of the best men who has ever lived on this earth.*

If you've ever experienced one of the Lord's tender mercies, you've been the recipient of a gift from a Heavenly Father who loves His children and who gives in ways that appear to be anonymous to those around us. When our lives are blessed and we don't even know who to thank, we can acknowledge the Lord's hand in all things and thank Him openly for these secret acts.

If the Lord asks us to serve one another anonymously, or "behind the scenes," we can be assured that the fruit of such service is always a measure of joy. And since the Lord at times asks us to serve anonymously, I think we can be assured He Himself finds joy in blessing us in ways we might not even recognize.

While we are considering the joys of Christmas, maybe we could consider blessing someone's life anonymously this season. As we learn from Scrooge, from Joseph, and from the Lord Himself, there is a special kind of joy that comes from giving in secret.

"I was just beginning to learn about this man, Jesus Christ, whose birthday we were celebrating. But it seemed like a pretty good deal. It was His birthday, but we got all the presents. What child didn't love that! Christmas was everything good. . . . As a child, I thought Christmas came just one day a year. As an adult, I now realize it is Christmas every day. Because of the benevolence of a loving Heavenly Father and a beloved Savior, Jesus Christ, we are the recipients of a continuous flow of heavenly gifts—every day. Heavenly gifts too numerous to mention."

—*Kevin R. Duncan*

CHAPTER THREE

THE JOY OF GIVING TO A FRIEND

*T*he Lord encouraged us in the Doctrine and Covenants to seek wisdom "out of the best books" (D&C 88:118). Would it be too much of a stretch to say that there are not only best books, but best plays, and (dare I say it) best movies available to us in the latter days?

We've already talked about a best book, *A Christmas Carol*, which has been turned into plays and movies dozens of times. To me, one of the "best movies" ever is the Christmas movie *It's a Wonderful Life*. You've probably seen the movie, in which George Bailey, played by Jimmy Stewart, gets to a point where he is actually contemplating taking his own life. Then he is shown by an angel how wonderful his life really is, and what the world and his neighbors would be like without him—what the world would be like if he had never been born.

The title of this movie is ironic. Everything in this man's life is falling apart. His business is bankrupt, there is a warrant out for his arrest, and he is financially worth more dead than alive. It's not a "wonderful life" at all, at least by outward appearances and most worldly measures. But in the end, even before he learns how his trials are going to be lifted, George realizes that his life has been worth living.

There's a scene in the movie—in fact, just a moment within a scene, a couple of seconds long—that became important and profound to me only after I was married. It's at the very end, when friends and neighbors are rushing to the Bailey home and putting their cash in a basket to save George. Suddenly the taxi driver, Ernie, quiets the crowd and reads a telegram just received from London:

> MR GOWER CABLED YOU NEED CASH STOP
> MY OFFICE INSTRUCTED TO ADVANCE
> YOU UP TO 25 THOUSAND DOLLARS STOP

HEE HAW AND MERRY CHRISTMAS
SAM WAINWRIGHT

I missed it as a child every time, but just as Ernie reads the words "Sam Wainwright," George casts a knowing glance at his wife, Mary. Wow. That little glance speaks volumes. Those eyes meeting across the room open a window into the heart of George Bailey.

As you may remember, when George was courting Mary, he was ready to take on the world. He promised Mary he was going to "lasso the moon" and pull it down for her. George was well aware that Mary could have married Sam Wainwright and been wealthy and prosperous, but instead she chose to marry a man whose life was not turning out at all the way he had planned, a man whose life was full of problems. How grateful George must have been that Mary stuck with him!

I often feel a similar tug at my heart when I look across the room at my wife, whom I successfully persuaded to marry me when I know she could have married so many others. I'll bet a lot of husbands feel as I do when they see George look at Mary in that moment.

As the movie ends, we realize that George's problems are far from over. He still runs a struggling business. He still lives in a "drafty old barn," as he calls it. He still sacrificed his dreams so his brother could go to college, and he sacrificed his career goals by remaining at the Bailey Brothers Building and Loan so that others in town could have a roof over their head. But in the end, he learns that no man is a failure who has friends. And what wonderful friends they were!

I like to think of myself as a good friend, but I admit that I'm no Sam Wainwright. I've never been in London or any other financial capital of the world managing my international business affairs. I'm not in the habit of forwarding $25,000 to friends in need at the drop of a hat. But wealth is not the point. Whether our contribution is small or large, each of us has something we can give.

When I think of the Sam Wainwrights of the world, I am reminded of one of my favorite quotations from President Spencer W. Kimball: "God does notice us, and he watches over us. But it is usually through another person that he meets our needs." God's love for us is generally not manifested through thunder and lightning, or through a spectacular miracle, or through anything outwardly supernatural, but through "another person" who comes to the rescue.

In George Bailey's case, it was a lot of other people who came together to rescue their friend, making *It's a Wonderful Life* the right title for that movie after all, ironic as it may appear at first.

"All Is Well" or "All Is, Uh, . . . Well?"

Speaking of confusing messages, as a child, I was often puzzled by a passage in the Book of Mormon that seemed to warn against using the phrase *all is well*: "Wo be unto him that crieth: All is well!" (2 Nephi 28:25).

That really baffled my little mind. "Okay, brothers and sisters, don't say 'All is well.'" Then, right after that, "Now, we will close by singing 'Come, Come, Ye Saints,' and really belt out the last verse, okay? *'Oh, how we'll make this chorus swell—All is well! All is well!'*"

Confused the Dickens out of me as a kid, you might say. Well, I finally figured it out. Nephi was not warning us against the exact words *all is well* as much as he was against the attitude of "all is well" during times of prosperity. We may be thinking that everything is fine all around when, spiritually speaking, things are not well. In other words, wo unto those who say, "Hey, the economy is good, we're prosperous, all is well, let's eat and drink and be merry."

Now, to the lyrics of "Come, Come, Ye Saints." By contrast, the pioneers were singing "all is well" when clearly all was *not* well, at least from a temporal perspective. Every morning they were burying loved ones on the frozen plains! All was not well physically, but spiritually they were choosing to see everything with an eternal perspective and to sing with gusto, "All is well," when clearly it was not. Even when facing death, they could sing, "And should we die before our journey's through, happy day! All is well!"

Took me a while, but I figured it out. The hymn wasn't written in opposition to Nephi's words, but to teach us to see the joy in life regardless of the circumstances.

It's a wonderful life? Well, very often it isn't, but look closer—with the proper perspective, it is. God lives and is watching over us, and friends are often dispatched to come to our rescue, and we feel the fruits and the joy of friendship.

A Man of Sorrows, Acquainted with Grief

To me, one of the most staggering statements in scripture was given to Joseph Smith in Liberty Jail, when the Lord said to His Prophet, "The Son of Man hath descended below them all. Art thou greater than he?" (D&C 122:8). It's amazing that the most perfect Being to ever live on earth was treated so imperfectly, and that He was willing to descend below all things.

He was the King of kings, but He was sold for the price of a slave. He was the Father of heaven and earth, yet He was born in a stable for animals. He was the greatest of all, yet He washed the feet of His disciples like a servant. He made the sick and afflicted whole, yet He was scourged and whipped and bruised for our iniquities. He allowed His life to be taken, but He has offered us eternal life. He wants to give us all He has, but He allows us to choose what we will receive.

Elder Neal A. Maxwell spoke of a few more of the ironies Jesus endured:

> For Jesus, in fact, irony began at His birth. Truly, He suffered the will of the Father "in all things from the beginning." (3 Ne. 11:11.) This whole earth became

Jesus' footstool (see Acts 7:49), but at Bethlehem there was "no room . . . in the inn" (Luke 2:7) and "no crib for his bed." (Hymns, 1985, no. 206.)

At the end, meek and lowly Jesus partook of the most bitter cup without becoming the least bitter. (See 3 Ne. 11:11; D&C 19:18–19.) The Most Innocent suffered the most. Yet the King of Kings did not break, even when some of His subjects did unto Him "as they listed." (D&C 49:6.) Christ's capacity to endure such irony was truly remarkable. . . .

In heaven, Christ's lofty name was determined to be the only name on earth offering salvation to all mankind. (See Acts 4:12; 2 Ne. 25:20; see also Abr. 3:27.) Yet the Mortal Messiah willingly lived so modestly, even, wrote Paul, as a person "of no reputation." (Philip. 2:7.)

You'll notice that in the Doctrine and Covenants, the Lord often refers to early members and leaders of the Church as "my servants." But you'll also notice that in the later sections He increasingly refers to them as "my friends." In the book of John, Jesus also refers to us as "friends" in these words:

Greater love hath no man than this, that a man lay down his life for his friends. . . . Henceforth I call you not servants; for the servant knoweth not what his lord doeth: but I have called you friends; for all things that I have heard of my Father I have made known unto you. (John 15:13, 15)

Jesus found joy in giving to us, His friends. Remarkably, He preferred to suffer Himself rather than to see us suffer: "For behold, I, God, have suffered these things for all, that they might not suffer if they would repent" (D&C 19:16). The Greatest of all suffered the greatest of all suffering so that we, His friends, would not have to. We have been offered the greatest gift imaginable from the greatest friend we could ever have.

"Keep an eternal perspective," we often say, but it's a lot easier to pronounce than it is to practice. An eternal perspective, one of the sweetest fruits of a testimony of Jesus Christ, allows us to see that life really is wonderful, even when it isn't. That "all is well," even when it isn't. And that because of Christ, we who are made partakers of "misery and wo" at times might also have joy.

"Is your schedule too packed? Are certain cultural traditions and pressures causing you undue stress and preventing you from receiving and reflecting the joy of Christ's birth? How might you simplify your calendar this Christmas and plan better for next? . . .

"Perhaps this year you don't send those Christmas cards, or you let go of some other media-inspired expectation you have of yourself. The cost in either time or money will take away some of your ability to focus on the Savior and feel His Christmas joy. . . .

"Perhaps this year you have a simplified Christmas with more homemade gifts and gifts of service because the pressure and cost of trying to buy it all is too great—and unnecessary—and it will take away some of your ability to focus on the Savior and feel His Christmas peace."

—*Patrick Kearon*

CHAPTER FOUR

THE JOY OF GIVING TO FAMILY

*P*resident Henry B. Eyring once observed, "Gift giving isn't easy. It's *hard* to give a gift with confidence. There are so many things that can go wrong." President Eyring concluded that the best gifts involve three things: empathy—the giver will feel what you feel; freeness in giving—the giver will really want to give; and sacrifice—the giver will take time, effort, and thought in the gift, but his or her return in joy will be great.

I believe I have learned some of these same lessons in the perfect laboratory: my home. Perhaps the best lesson I've learned in giving to family members is this: *often the least expensive gifts are the most appreciated.*

Gifts that cost a lot of money are one thing; gifts that cost a lot in time, effort, and thought are another.

On our second Christmas together, I gave my wife a piece of paper. It was a rather large piece, about eighteen by twenty inches. What a gift, huh? Oh, and another thing—there was a lot of graphite on it. I spent hours and hours drawing, erasing, and blending, followed by more drawing, erasing, and blending. Several times I almost got caught in the act of drawing, erasing, and blending, and I had to quickly stash the paper under a blanket and pretend I was doing something else.

Then another event nearly blew my cover and spoiled my surprise. One day Kim took messages off the answering machine, including one from an employee at the frame shop, who called to tell me, "Your frame is ready." My wife heard the whole thing and kept mum, but I knew she suspected something. So I devised a stratagem—I left a few of her as-yet-unframed Church paintings on the washer to try to send her suspicion sideways. (It worked.)

Finally, my drawing was done, inserted into its modest frame, wrapped, and placed beneath the tree. I had never been more excited about a gift in my life!

I planned it all out so that it would be the last one she opened—for maximum effect. As our newlywed Christmas morning was winding down, Kim picked up this last gift, knowing by its rectangular shape that it was some sort of framed picture. She slowly pulled the wrapping paper back, expecting to see one of her Church paintings. Instead, she saw my drawing of her own smiling face looking back at her. She paused. She stared. She looked stunned, and then she began to cry. Watching her reaction, I got a little emotional myself. Was it because the drawing looked good, or because it looked bad? (To this day, I'm not really sure.)

What I *am* sure about is that she appreciated the gift because she knew that piece of paper represented a lot of time, effort, and thought. Actions speak louder than words? Absolutely. Time, effort, and thought say "I love you!" with a little thunder instead of just letters on a card. I told her how much fun it had been to look at a photograph of her beautiful face nearly every day for a few weeks while trying to reproduce it in pencil. I could have bought a ring, a necklace, a bracelet, or any number of much more expensive items, and the financial transaction would have been complete in a

matter of seconds, but it wouldn't have been the same. It wouldn't have been as good. Not even close. Lesson learned with impact: *the least expensive gifts are often the most appreciated.*

Anticipating the Recipient's Reaction

We've tried to teach our children the same thing. Each December, part of our family tradition includes reading the classic story by Pearl S. Buck titled *Christmas Day in the Morning*. In a nutshell, a young boy on the farm decides to wake up early and do the morning chores as a gift for his father. The moment that I love—and the moment that I want my children to see and appreciate—is that as the boy begins to milk the cow, a chore that he normally despises, he is giddy with excitement. His anticipation of how his father will react when seeing the chores are already done fills him with joy. In that moment, work doesn't seem like work and time seems to fly. That's the spirit of Christmas.

The gift this boy gave his father wasn't wrapped in a package, and it wasn't purchased with money. Those kinds of gifts are easy, especially today. Just buy a gift card online and be done with the whole thing in a few clicks. This boy's gift wasn't convenient, and it wasn't easy. It was a gift of self and a gift of time, and when you're giving someone your time, it's a gift only you can give. You can't buy that on Amazon!

You Can't Steal Christmas

Another Christmas movie with a great family message is *How the Grinch Stole Christmas*—not the newer one featuring famous actors and elaborate costumes, but the old Dr. Seuss cartoon version.

We all know the story of the Grinch, who under the cover of darkness snuck into town disguised as

Santa Claus and stole all the Christmas presents, trees, and food. We also remember that when all the Whos in Whoville woke up and found their Christmas was gone, they just did what they had always done. They assembled in the town square, held hands in a huge circle, and began to sing. They knew that Christmas—the holiday, but more important, the feeling—was still within their grasp. Why? Because they had hands to clasp. They were together. They had each other.

Did I absorb that lofty, selfless message as a child? Nope. Not at all. In fact, I remember being a little confused watching all the Whos in Whoville smiling and singing. Could you really be happy and hold hands and sing when your Christmas had been stolen? The Christmas you had been anticipating for months? All the presents, all the decorations, the tree, and the feast, gone? Could you really act as if nothing had happened when you didn't even have your last can of Who Hash? I wasn't sure. But that was exactly the point the movie was trying to make. You can steal Christmas gifts, yes. But you can't steal Christmas. Christmas isn't gifts. Christmas is the people around you.

Your Presents and Your Presence

Many years ago, as a recently returned missionary, I remember looking across the room at my dad, who was approaching the age of seventy. I was pondering the fact that the most important people to him in that moment were surrounding him: his wife, children, and grandchildren, fully engaged in the noise and chaos of a level-one Christmas celebration.

It also occurred to me that if I could fast-forward my life and take a peek at myself fifty years hence, I hoped the same thing would be true for me. I thought to myself, *The people who will be most important to me when I'm in my seventies aren't even here yet.* That was an interesting thought. I could hardly wait to meet these people (especially my future wife)!

Well, I did meet her, and, one by one, the children arrived. A couple of decades later, there was a moment on Christmas Day when I felt the wonderful kind of joy my father must have felt. It didn't involve tangible gifts, but that Christmas morning of 2018 spread across three different countries on two continents and an island: the United States, France, and Iceland.

My two oldest children were on missions, and

they both called home on Christmas morning. What made it even more fun was the technology. It wasn't just a phone call but a video call. I could see their excited expressions from across the Atlantic Ocean right there on my wife's phone! We were so excited to talk to them, but as it turned out, the best part of the call was when we were not talking at all. My wife and I listened and marveled as our missionaries talked to *each other*, encouraged each other, and counseled with each other about their challenges and their missions. I was so struck by how incredible it was that I took a photo.

Our family was able to clasp hands across the world using technology. No gift under the tree could have compared with that phone call.

What a gift, and what a morning! We spoke of Christ and of Christmas, and although no gifts were exchanged, the most important people to me were right there. That was what made that particular Christmas morning unforgettable. Their presence trumped their presents.

Lying in a Manger

The first Christmas was a family event, the story of the birth of a king—and not just any king, but the *King* of kings. The Book of Mormon calls Him by such exalted titles as "the Lord Omnipotent" (Mosiah 3:5) and "the Father of heaven and of earth" (Helaman 14:12). Isaiah calls Him "The mighty God, The everlasting Father, The Prince of Peace" (Isaiah 9:6).

Sometimes we sing "I Stand All Amazed," and in our best moments, we really are amazed at the love Jesus offers us. On other occasions, we sing "Jesus, Once of Humble Birth." If we combine the two titles, we *stand all amazed at Jesus's humble birth*. Perhaps the circumstances of Jesus's birth are just another way He "descended below all things" (D&C 88:6).

And, stunningly, the shepherds are told they will

find him "lying in a *manger*" (Luke 2:12; emphasis added). Not a castle, not a palace, not a throne room, no. It won't look wonderful, comfortable, or opulent. It won't be clean and tidy and free from strange animal smells. Joseph and Mary will be in a rush to pay their taxes, probably very stressed and tired from a long journey. To add to the difficulty of the situation, there will be no room for them at the inn, and (how much more lowly could it be?) you will find the King of kings and Lord of lords lying in a *manger*.

There you will find this little, holy family most certainly feeling the joy of what has just happened, since both Mary and Joseph have been taught that from this humble beginning, the Messiah will come into the world.

As mentioned earlier, President Eyring observed that the best gifts involve three things: empathy—the giver will feel what you feel; freeness in giving—the giver will really want to give; and sacrifice—the giver will take time, effort, and thought in the gift, knowing the return in joy will be great. President Eyring concluded, "God, the Father, gave his Son, and Jesus

Christ gave us the Atonement, the greatest of all gifts and all giving."

Lying in a manger on that first Christmas was the Christ child, who would perfectly embody these three principles:

EMPATHY: Jesus came to feel what we would feel (see Alma 7:11–12).

FREENESS IN GIVING: Jesus came to give His life freely (see John 10:17–18).

SACRIFICE: Jesus came to suffer so that we might not suffer (see D&C 19:16).

God so loved the world that He gave His Son, and Jesus so loved us that He gave His life. These stunning gifts fill us with joy, and because of these gifts, we can repent, change, grow, and become. And when we repent, we create joy in heaven (see Luke 15:7, 10).

"At the moment of depression, if you will follow a simple program, you will get out of it. Get on your knees and get the help of God; then get up and go find somebody who needs something that you can help them find. Then it will be a good day."

—*Marion D. Hanks*

CHAPTER FIVE

THE JOY OF GIVING SPONTANEOUSLY

A number of years ago, I stopped to fill up my car with gas at a local Tesoro station. While I was leaning against my fender, watching the numbers on the pump, a woman approached me who was filling her car in the lane next to me. I tensed up a little, thinking she was going to ask me for money, but she didn't. She said, "Excuse me, sir, do you know much about tires?" "A little," I responded. She pointed at her tires and asked, "Do you think these tires can make it to Ogden?"

I looked, and my first thought was, *Uh, I don't think they can make it to I-15.* I couldn't believe the tires on her car were even holding air. The sides were so badly bulging and worn that the cords or strings or whatever tires are made of were sticking out. And that was just the sides! What did the tread look like? I shudder to think. I just knew I wouldn't put anyone I cared about in a car with tires like that.

Now, she could not have known this little fact about me: I happen to be a bit crazy when it comes to tires. I bought some lousy tires in college, and after two or three trips back to the tire shop trying to get my car to stop pulling to the right or left and just go straight, I called my dad, who simply said, "John—don't compromise on tires." Good tires make a big difference. Today, one of my favorite sensations is driving on new tires. Aren't I odd?

Anyway, I don't know what came over me that fall afternoon, but I got in my car and told her to follow me. She did, and we drove a few blocks down Highland Drive until I pulled into a Firestone Tires service center. We walked inside, and, as I tugged at my wallet, I asked the manager, "What would it take to put some decent tires on that car? She needs to get to Ogden." He looked at me, and then at the woman and her friend (who was starting to cry), then back at me.

After a brief discussion about the cost, he also sensed the situation at hand. He gave us both a wink and said, "We'll throw in a free oil change, too."

As we were waiting, the woman told me that she and her traveling companion were going to see a sick friend in Ogden but they had started worrying about whether they could make it. As I heard her story, my heart softened even more, and while she stayed there to wait for her new tires, I made a quick trip to the ATM to give her a little insurance money.

I got back just in time to see the manager pull her car out and hand her the keys. Then something occurred that I don't recall ever happening to me before. She thanked me, hugged me, and called me an angel. I still remember the feeling I had as she and her friend drove away.

Now, I may have just forfeited any blessing I received from that event by telling you all about it, but I'll risk it, because I just have to say—I was filled to overflowing with a feeling of joy and satisfaction that I had rarely felt before. And the strange thing is, it lasted for days and days and days. I feel a portion of it again as I try to explain it now. I've heard the promise thousands of times, and so have you: it is more blessed to give than to receive. I must concur. I was blessed beyond anything I could have expected.

In fact, this experience reminds me of a song. We had dozens of Christmas records at my house when I was growing up, and, coincidentally, some of them were Firestone Christmas albums from the 1960s. (Does anyone out there remember those?) The Firestone Tire Company commissioned several Christmas albums (they're all on YouTube now). One of our favorite Firestone Christmas albums has a delightful arrangement of the song "Sleigh Ride." There is a line in the chorus that I probably heard a million times as a kid. It says, "There's a happy feeling nothing in the world can buy . . ."

I have thought about that phrase a lot. There really is a happy feeling out there that cannot be bought. Nothing in the world could have given me that feeling, that Christmas feeling. I could have hired a team of life coaches, or read a dozen self-help books, or disappeared into the desert to find myself, and never discovered that feeling. Nothing in the world can buy it, but the mysterious thing is, it can be received by giving.

This woman who drove away sporting new tires on a beat-up Ford Tempo called me an angel. Was I? No. Not even close. I was just a guy with a Visa card who loves new tires, but I have to tell you—playing the angel role sure felt good. Really good. The Tesoro station where my little story took place is now a vacant lot, and the Firestone Tire store is vacant as well, but whenever I pass by, the pleasant memory returns (and sometimes I hear the faint sound of jingle bells).

Today, there's someone out there—a neighbor, a friend, a ward member—trying to move forward on really bad tires. They could have a blowout at any moment. Their tires could be emotional, spiritual, or physical (or they could actually be tires).

A sister at a Time Out for Women conference showed me a message on her phone that she had programmed to appear each day as she awoke: "Who needs me today?" Those words popped up every morning, and she would pause and ponder the question and wait for some inspiration. Notice, her reminder wasn't to ask herself, *Does* anyone need me today? Her assumption was, For sure, someone does. There are a lot of bad tires out there. Her question was, *Who* needs me today? And every day, this awesome sister would act. That's what honorary angels do. A note, a call, a text, a visit—she would find someone and give something. Perhaps we might discover the joy of spontaneous giving every day if we were to ask the same question.

I am reminded of how often Jesus stopped to bless people when He was actually heading somewhere else. When He was on His way to see the daughter of Jairus, another daughter who had struggled for twelve years with an issue of blood reached out and touched the hem of His garment. She wasn't on Jesus's to-do list. He was on His way to fulfill a different task, but suddenly, someone needed Him. He stopped, He looked, He listened, He stayed (see Mark 5:24–35). He healed, blessed, and encouraged this woman before going on His way. Such opportunities may come to us, interrupting the task at hand with another task—but both tasks are opportunities, and even the tasks not on our to-do lists are important!

A number of years ago, a reporter was visiting with President Thomas S. Monson just prior to his birthday, and at the conclusion of the interview, the reporter asked President Monson what he would consider the ideal gift that Church members worldwide could give to him. President Monson replied, "Find someone who is having a hard time or is ill or lonely, and do something for him or her."

After his birthday had passed, President Monson said that he received hundreds of birthday cards and notes from members of the Church reporting how they had fulfilled his request. Even Primary children sent reports in various forms, including a jar full of "warm fuzzies," each fuzzy representing an act of service.

When I remember the service of President Monson, I always think of the hymn "Have I Done Any Good?" And I must confess, it's easy for me to pack my bags for a guilt trip when I sing that song and realize that most of what I do each day benefits only me and my family. That's why I like the word *today* in the song.

> *There are chances for work all around just now,*
> *Opportunities right in our way.*
> *Do not let them pass by, saying, "Sometime I'll try,"*
> *But go and do something today.*

Yesterday's gone, and I can't do anything about that. But even if I have regrets about yesterday and all the things I coulda shoulda and woulda done, I don't have to let them stop me from thinking of something I can do *today*—even if it's as simple as a text message containing an encouraging word or an expression of gratitude. We should never let regrets about yesterday stop us from doing something today!

The longer I live, the more I see the hand of the Lord in placing each of us in circles where we can bless and be there for one another. Somehow, the Lord arranged for the wise men not only to see a star but to know what it meant, and to travel some distance to inquire about "the child that is born, the Messiah of the Jews" (JST, Matthew 2:2). Elder Neal A. Maxwell observed:

> *The same God that placed that star in a precise orbit millennia before it appeared over Bethlehem in celebration of the birth of the Babe has given at least equal attention to placement of each of us in precise human orbits so that we may, if we will, illuminate the landscape of our individual lives, so that our light may not only lead others but warm them as well.*

I believe the Lord may place us in "orbits" so that you and I may be a light, be a friend, and serve in such a way that we may capture that "happy feeling nothing in the world can buy."

"Using one internet search engine, I found thousands of items advertised with the phrase 'The gift that never stops giving.' Yet try as we may, no *material* gift that we give will last forever. . . . Wouldn't a gift that never stops giving be considered a perfect gift? First, a perfect gift would reveal something about the giver of the gift. Second, it would reflect something about the needs of the person receiving the gift. And finally, the gift, if it was really the perfect gift, would hold its value not just as time goes on but forever. . . . I testify that Jesus Christ is the perfect gift—the gift that never stops giving."

—*Joy D. Jones*

CHAPTER SIX

THE JOY OF RECEIVING GOD'S GIFTS

One holiday season, I found myself in the tropics of the Philippines watching—believe it or not—snow falling from the sky. "Snow in the Philippines?" you may be asking. "Was it some sort of unusual weather phenomenon?" No. I was in the conference room of a hotel surrounded by other missionaries of the Philippines Baguio (BAG-ee-oh) Mission at our Christmas conference. Sitting beside me was one of my high school friends who had been called to the same mission. Suddenly we found ourselves watching the snow falling on our hometown of Salt Lake City in the movie *Mr. Krueger's Christmas*. We could see on the screen something familiar to us both: Temple Square was aglow with lights, and the cold, white stuff was gently blanketing the ground while the dancers danced and the Tabernacle Choir sang carols.

I looked at Elder Chris Andrew, and he looked at me, and we both thought, *Uh, I'm not sure I wanna keep watching this . . . getting a little homesick here, thinking of my hometown, my home, and my family's tradition of going downtown to see the lights.*

Well, we had a wonderful Christmas conference and eventually said good-bye to all the other missionaries. I grabbed my regular companion, got back on a bus, and returned to our own area. We spent Christmas Day that year doing what we normally did on every other day—walking around talking to people about the Savior and His gospel.

Then, something happened a few days later that I still can't quite wrap my head around. It was as if I received a Christmas card from God. Somehow, the Lord brought a piece of Temple Square to a little barrio in the Philippines. I have never seen anything like it, before or since, but one night, while walking back to our apartment in the hot, muggy Philippine climate, my companion and I turned the corner and discovered a tree absolutely glistening with thousands of fireflies. It was not an evergreen tree, but it didn't matter—it was twinkling as beautifully as anything on Temple Square, half a world away. Lots of people were standing around looking at the tree in awe, which told me that what we were seeing really was unusual, that this sort of thing didn't happen very often. In my partially homesick state during my very first Christmas season away from home, I wondered, *Did God do that for me?*

Then a little argument began in my head: "Oh, come on, John, you're not anywhere near that important. This is just a coincidence." Of course I wasn't that important, but—was it possible? This was a spiritual tug of war for me: on one side, thinking I was more important than I am (which I didn't want to do), and on the other side, acknowledging the Lord's hand in all things (which I knew I must do). Perhaps my mom and dad had been praying that I would not be homesick, and the Lord had steered my path toward that spectacular firefly convention just to let me know He was there. Could it be?

Someone once said, "Coincidences are God's way of remaining anonymous." I don't know. But I thought it wise to thank the Lord for making it happen, just in case. I will never forget Christmas on my mission, my very first Christmas away from home, and I will never forget this little tender mercy.

Does the Lord keep careful track of our comings and goings? Does He care what we're up to, and does He watch over us as we move about? Or is that work delegated to angels, or perhaps to our loved ones on the other side of the veil acting in an angelic capacity? I wonder.

I've Got Eyes on You

I remember fulfilling a speaking assignment at BYU one night in early April, getting to my car about nine p.m., and heading straight for Vernal, Utah (normally a two-hour drive), where I had a school assembly to give the next morning. I drove up Provo Canyon and proceeded east out of Heber City on Highway 40. Then, suddenly, it began to snow. Hard. Added to that, it was about ten p.m. and was getting cold. I could hardly see the road in front of me. This was one of those snowstorms in which flipping on your high-beam lights made it not better but much worse.

I slowed down, but I was nervous that someone behind me would not slow down and, not seeing me, would hit me from behind. I was also concerned that there might be someone in front of me going even more slowly than I was. I felt like I was driving inside a giant snow globe after a vigorous shaking. I could see only about twenty to thirty feet in front of me, and I carefully watched the lines in the center of the highway go by on my left, with no idea where I was outside that little bubble.

Suddenly, I felt my flip-phone buzz, and my wife texted two words, "You okay?" I was, but I didn't want to take my hands off the wheel to text a reply (this was before Siri could help). White-knuckled and concentrating intensely on the road in front of me, I prayed, "Heavenly Father, I don't really care how long this takes, just help me get there safely."

Suddenly I had the thought, "Turn on your GPS." Today, GPS technology is integrated into our phones, but back when this happened, GPS devices were separate little units, and mine was attached to my windshield. I reached over and hit the power button, and wow, what a difference it made. The little screen lit up from the viewpoint of one looking down from above. Immediately, I saw the road I was on, the direction I was going, even some of my surroundings!

I could see that Highway 40 was about to begin a gentle turn to the left, and that Strawberry Reservoir was off the highway to my right—things I could not see by looking out my windshield. Having driven this route to Vernal numerous times before in the daylight, I now had a good sense of about where I was from my GPS, and that was such a relief, because all I could see with my natural eyes was a blizzard, and I was just

working hard to hug those lines on my left going past me and dividing the highway.

How interesting, I thought as I progressed down the snowy highway. A bunch of satellites above seemed to be whispering, "You're okay, we gotcha. You've got hundreds of eyes on you that you didn't even know were there. Don't worry. We're watching." I still had a long drive ahead, but I knew where I was in my route, and my spirit relaxed a bit.

The experience reminded me of a remarkable statement of President John Taylor:

God lives, and his eyes are over us, and his angels are round and about us, and they are more interested in us than we are in ourselves, ten thousand times, but we do not know it.

If the angels of God really are interested in us, not just a little, but ten thousand times more interested than we are in ourselves (which is amazing—we've all known people who seemed to be very interested in themselves), then perhaps God really does watch over us, and He sends us tender mercies along the way.

On This Night Will the Sign Be Given

We often think of the Christmas tradition of giving gifts as having originated with the wise men who brought gold, frankincense, and myrrh to the Christ child.

But consider the story in Third Nephi, the story of Christmas in the New World. Nephi (son of Nephi) had heard the prophecy of Samuel the Lamanite. Samuel, rather than saying something nebulous like "in the future" or "the time is near," had been extremely specific: "Five more years cometh, and behold, then cometh the Son of God" among men (Helaman

14:2). Unbelievers also heard Samuel's prophecy, and you'd better believe they wrote it down. They kept track. They counted every month as the time passed, and when it got to five years, they became very loud and vocal about the fact that the five years were up. They celebrated. They mocked. They enjoyed the misfortune of others, and they were rude:

> *And they began to rejoice over their brethren, saying: Behold the time is past, and the words of Samuel are not fulfilled; therefore, your joy and your faith concerning this thing hath been vain. And it came to pass that they did make a great uproar throughout the land. (3 Nephi 1:6–7)*

They clearly assumed the believers' faith had been in vain, perhaps a lesson for us in the last days as we might begin to wonder if the Lord is "delay[ing] his coming" (D&C 45:26).

The Nephite prophet at the time was Nephi son of Nephi (or, as the index calls him, Nephi³). Nephi saw all of this, and he went out to pray. Oh, how I would love to know what he said, and how long he prayed! I imagine somewhere in that prayer was something like this: "Lord, we need the sign. We need it tonight. They have set aside a day to put all the believers to death. And if we have to die, I guess that's okay; just wanted you to know . . ."

(Parenthetically, I have often wondered what kind of system was in place that allowed the killing of people for holding a particular belief. All we know is that the Gadianton robbers filled the judgment-seats, so freedom of religion was not a protected right [see Helaman 7:4]).

Now, what if you were a believer? What if you were a believer with children? What would you tell them? "Kids, uh, it could be tomorrow that they will ask us whether we believe or not. What should we do?" Elder David A. Bednar commented on the precarious situation of these believers:

> *Brothers and sisters, can we even begin to understand what it might have been like to await the sign of His coming and also face the dire deadline of death? Would you and I stand firm and steadfast in the faith, or would we waver and shrink?*

Perhaps you'd have a private conversation with your spouse, "Honey, what if they kill us but make slaves of our children? Perhaps we should deny our beliefs to save them. What should we do?" We can only imagine the intensity of the situation for these families. No wonder Nephi prayed "all that day" (3 Nephi 1:12).

Finally, the answer came. (Isn't it interesting how the Lord often waits until the last minute?)

> *And it came to pass that he cried mightily unto the Lord all that day; and behold, the voice of the Lord came unto him, saying: Lift up your head and be of good cheer; for behold, the time is at hand, and on this night shall the sign be given, and on the morrow come I into the world. (3 Nephi 1:12–13)*

It was as if the Lord were saying, "Nephi, the sign will come tonight. Don't be afraid. I'm coming. Now go let everyone know." So perhaps we could say with confidence that Jesus Himself was the first to give gifts on the night of His own birth: "The sign will come tonight, and you can all live."

I've tried to imagine those believers watching the sunset, wondering if it would be their last. Then I've imagined their astonishment after the going down of the sun, when they realized it wasn't getting any darker.

Ten minutes. Then twenty minutes. Then thirty minutes. Then an hour or two! I'll bet they had either fallen to their knees or were dancing in the streets. Maybe a little of both! Elder Bednar continued:

The day Jesus was born was a day of deliverance for the believers in the New World. Light as the sign of the Savior's birth literally saved their lives.

The Light of the World had come to earth, and the believers must have been filled with joy knowing that they would all live because Jesus came on that night. What night was it? Christmas Eve. The Light had come, just as Samuel the Lamanite had prophesied! Elder Bednar concluded:

Many of our memorable and enduring Christmas traditions include different kinds of lights—lights on trees, lights in and on our homes, candles on our tables. May the beautiful lights of every holiday season remind us of Him who is the source of all light.

When I reflect on the many different kinds of light we enjoy at Christmastime, I personally add a couple of items that remind me of the Lord's tender mercies—fireflies and GPS devices.

We all know that one of Jesus's titles is "the Light of the World," and amazingly, He shares that name with us. When He appeared in the New World, He said, "*I* am the light and the life of the world" (3 Nephi 11:11); but in Matthew 5:14, He said, "*Ye* are the light of the world." Jesus explained how His light and our light can work together: "Therefore, hold up your light that it may shine unto the world. Behold I am the light which ye shall hold up—that which ye have seen me do" (3 Nephi 18:24). Just another of God's gifts that we receive is the opportunity to join Him in the joyous mission of bringing His light to the world.

"Jesus Christ will repair every bad note and redeem every sour overtone if we turn to Him and ask for His help. Because of the birth, the Atonement, and the Resurrection of Jesus Christ, we can all 'sleep in heavenly peace.'"

—*Sharon Eubank*

CHAPTER SEVEN

THE JOY OF FORGIVING AND RECEIVING

*Y*ears ago, the Church produced a movie called *Nora's Christmas Gift,* about a woman who was experiencing the perils of aging. She had been a super-woman, doing everything for everyone, but she was losing her eyesight and struggling to maintain the pace she had been used to. Her friends were trying to help her, accept her, and love her, but she retreated into her own depression.

Something happened to Nora, though, when she recognized some profound counsel hidden within the lyrics of the Christmas carol "Joy to the World." The life-changing phrase for Nora was, "Let earth receive her king." She realized she had never learned to receive.

She was the one organizing the service projects, not the focus of them. She was too independent, too self-sufficient before, but she learned that there comes a time for all of us to learn to receive.

One of the things most of us need to learn to receive is forgiveness. (We need to give it, too.) You'll notice the word *give* is part of the word *forgive*, and we can all give that gift when we receive an apology and are able to say, "I accept your apology" or, "You're forgiven; don't give it another thought."

A Lesson in Forgiving

My friend Barbara taught me about forgiving in a profound way. My family moved across town just before I turned thirteen, and when I began classes at Hillside Intermediate School, I had no friends there. So, in my seventh-grade English class, when the buzz around the room about a month after school started was that "Barbara was coming back," I didn't know what people were talking about. I didn't know what had happened to Barbara, or why everyone was so excited, but I soon found out. Barbara had been walking down the sidewalk when a car had jumped the curb and hit her, damaging her leg to the point that, after enduring thirty-five surgeries and nine months in the hospital, she had finally had to have it amputated.

Barbara came back to school with a pretty noticeable limp and a prosthetic leg, but she smiled through the whole thing. Her friends and Young Women leaders helped her rebuild her life, teaching her, as she later said, "how to ride a bike, to play tennis, and just to laugh again." I admired Barbara from afar; I felt she was a little out of my league back then. She even had a short piece published about her experience, a couple of years after her accident, in the December 1977 *New Era.*

I've kept in touch with Barbara over the years (she happens to live in my mother's ward), and I'm happy to report that, despite her early fears that "no man would choose a wife like me," she married a great returned missionary named Jon, and they have five children.

Many years later, while serving as the Relief Society president in my mother's ward, Barbara shared a sacred experience that brings her story full circle, a story I will never forget. She said that after the accident, occasionally she would hear her parents whisper about someone named Ann. Ann was the person who had been driving the car that had hit and injured Barbara so severely.

Sometimes Barbara's family would see Ann in the neighborhood, or at the store, but they avoided her and never spoke to her. After graduating from high school, Barbara even worked at a hospital where Ann was also employed, and occasionally she would see Ann in the hall, but they never talked.

Years passed—nearly three decades, in fact—and Barbara began to think more and more about Ann. She wondered how Ann was doing, how her life had unfolded. Acting on a prompting, Barbara opened the phone book and began to search. Grateful to find that Ann's name was there, Barbara gave her a call. She told Ann who she was and asked if she could maybe come visit with her that day. The phone went silent. Eventually Ann spoke, and she halfheartedly agreed. Barbara gathered up some pictures of her family and drove to Ann's house, nervous, yet excited.

Barbara describes what happened when she rang the doorbell:

The woman I knew as Ann, only now much older (probably in her late seventies), came to the door. She did not invite me in; instead, she invited me to sit on the front porch. I instantly realized that she was very nervous and scared of me. She wanted to know what I wanted from her.

I reassured her that I was only there to tell her something I had wanted to say for many years. I told her, "I want you to know that I know what happened that day in January 1975 was an accident." I said that I had no hard feelings for her and that my life was great and I was very happy. I really was fine.

She told me of her hard, hard life: her husband had died young, leaving her with only one child, a son who was mentally handicapped. That accident had practically destroyed her.

She and I talked and talked, and we both cried. At some point in the conversation I asked her why she had never one time come to see me or even call me after the accident. I told her that, as a child, I had been taught that when you hurt someone, you should tell them, "I'm sorry." It had been hard for me to understand why she never did that. She told me she had been told by her attorneys not to speak to me, as that would imply an admission of guilt. She told me that she had called the hospital many times and asked how I was doing.

When we finished our conversation, Ann looked me in the eye and said, "Now I can die. I feel content with my life." I told her that I didn't want her to die, but that I felt such a lift as well. I had spent about an hour enveloped in some of the most tender feelings of my life. It was the closest thing to the pure love of Christ I had ever felt. I have since come to realize and appreciate that feeling as charity.

I will never forget that experience sitting on a bench on a little front porch with a woman whom I really had never known, yet who had occupied my thoughts for so many years. Walls had come down; barriers had been broken for both of us.

Could Ann's life have been happier had I come long before now? What if she had passed away before I finally got around to calling? As a young girl, all I could think about was, "Why doesn't she come or call and say she is sorry? She should be the one to call me— she caused the accident." As an adult, my heart ached for the pain, suffering, and guilt she most certainly had been feeling for so many years. Why did it take me so long to forgive?

Barbara's story has blessed my life. To paraphrase a dozen or so scriptures, if the Lord is willing to forgive us, how we ought to forgive one another. "Such mercy, such love and devotion can I forget?" The Lord is eager to forgive. What a gift, so freely given!

The Lord's Prayer teaches us the phrase "Forgive us our debts, *as we forgive our debtors*" (Matthew 6:12; emphasis added). In other words, we need to forgive others if we expect to obtain forgiveness. But shouldn't it be all right to wait until others ask for forgiveness before we extend it? The Prophet Joseph Smith observed, "Should we even forgive our brother, or even our enemy, before he repent or ask forgiveness, our heavenly Father would be equally as merciful unto us."

Welcome Home

The level-one Christmas movie *Home Alone* includes such a nice forgiveness story that President Thomas S. Monson made mention of it in a general conference address. The movie features Macaulay Culkin as Kevin, a little boy who is accidentally left "home alone" when his family departs for a European vacation. In one scene, Kevin meets his neighbor, an old man who previously has been a frightening mystery. Kevin asks the man if he has any family, and the man replies that he does have a son, but that he is estranged from that son and his family. President Monson related:

In the innocence of youth, the boy blurts out the plea, "Why don't you just call your son and tell him you are sorry and invite him home for Christmas!"

The old man sighs and responds, "I'm too afraid he would say no." The fear of failure had blocked the ability to express love and to voice an apology.

The viewer is left to wonder concerning the outcome of the conversation, but not for too long. Christmas comes; the boy's family returns. He is pictured at an upstairs bedroom window looking in the direction of the old man's sidewalk. Suddenly he views a tender scene as the neighbor welcomes his returning son, his daughter-in-law, and their children. Son embraces father, and the old man buries his head against the shoulder of his precious son. As they turn to walk on, the old neighbor looks upward to the bedroom window of the house next door and sees his small friend observing the private miracle of forgiveness. Their eyes meet, their hands express a gentle greeting of gratitude. "Welcome home" replaces "Home alone."

One emerges from the theater with moist eyes. As the brightness of day envelops the silent throng, perhaps there are those whose thoughts turn to that man of miracles, that teacher of truth—even the Lord of lords, Jesus Christ. I know my thoughts did.

Each Christmas, we are led to ask ourselves, is there anyone I need to forgive? Are there any grudges I need to let go of or judgments I need to withhold and repent of? Is there anyone I need to apologize to, anyone I have offended, intentionally or not, that I can reach out to? Are there fences I need to mend?

The First Presidency included forgiveness in their 2018 description of four of Jesus's gifts to us: "Our Savior, Jesus Christ, offers to us four incomparable gifts—the capacity to love others, the ability to forgive, the blessing of repentance, and the promise of life everlasting. These four unique gifts will bring us more and more joy as we accept and act upon them."

May we each give forgiveness and receive forgiveness. More important, may we each "receive our King" and His incomparable gifts—including the gift of Christmas joy.

"At this time of year we celebrate the birth of our Savior, Jesus Christ. His life was the greatest life ever lived.

"Even in secular terms, His life has had greater impact on every part of this world and its history than any life ever lived.

"No one who has ever lived has more monuments to His life and teaching than He. . . . The greatest art and music of the Western world has been devoted to celebrating the birth and the life and the mission of Jesus Christ.

"Kingdoms have been founded and overthrown to serve His purposes, as the leaders of that time supposed. Armies have marched and navies have put to sea and continents have been discovered and populated.

"Philosophers and theologians have spent their lives studying His teachings. Among other impacts, those teachings have unquestionably fostered political systems that dignify and provide rights to the individual and have inspired charity, education, and culture.

"Millions have given their lives, and, more importantly, millions have patterned their lives after the Lord God of Israel, Jehovah, Jesus Christ, our Savior."

—*Dallin H. Oaks*

CHAPTER EIGHT

JOY IN GOD
OUR SAVIOR

*M*uch has been written and spoken about Mary, the mother of Jesus. How can we possibly overestimate her influence? Elder Gerald N. Lund has written:

> *Mary's contribution to the church and to the work of Jesus Christ may be more lasting than most people realize. . . . She contributed to the training of her son Jesus. Her knowledge of the scriptures was thorough, as indicated by her spontaneous words of rejoicing when she met Elizabeth, words that echo numerous passages in the Old Testament (Luke 1:46–55).*

Mary was mentioned in the Book of Mormon by

King Benjamin, who knew that her name would be Mary more than a hundred years before she was born. Alma also spoke of Mary to the people in Gideon, describing her as "a precious and chosen vessel" about eighty-three years before she was born (Alma 7:10). Clearly her mission was foreordained, as Elder Bruce R. McConkie testified:

> *There was only one Christ, and there is only one Mary. Each was noble and great in preexistence, and each was foreordained to the ministry he or she performed. We cannot but think that the Father would choose the greatest female spirit to be the mother of his Son, even as he chose the male spirit like unto him to be the Savior.*

Here's a question you've probably never been asked: What do Nephi (son of Lehi) and Mary (the mother of Jesus) have in common? Nephi lived long before Mary, likely being a teenager in 600 BC. Some six centuries later, Mary was also likely a teenager when espoused to Joseph and visited by the angel Gabriel. Other than their being very young when we first hear about them, they don't really have much in common, do they?

After Nephi lost his father, Lehi, arguably one of his closest friends, he lamented, "O wretched man that I am!" (2 Nephi 4:17). Most of us would not think of Nephi as "wretched" at all. Interestingly, what might be called a low point for him emotionally was one of Nephi's greatest moments. If we *always* "feel good about ourselves," that's a problem. Each of us desperately needs the Savior. Nephi was probably thinking of the times when he was angry with his brothers, and his self-described "wretchedness" led him to remember his reliance on God, which he expressed in a poetic way. In fact, 2 Nephi 4 has been called the "Psalm of Nephi" because it sounds like an ancient psalm, a song of praise to the Lord.

Mary, after being visited by Gabriel, also offered something like a psalm. It has been called the "Magnificat" because of Mary's expression, "My soul doth *magnify* the Lord" (Luke 1:46; emphasis added). Mary's psalm is evidence of her abundant knowledge of the scriptures, since many of the phrases she used have Old Testament roots.

Nephi in a time of turmoil and Mary in a time of rejoicing each offered a psalm of praise. If we place their words side by side, we notice their focus on the source of their faith, their hope, and their power to endure.

NEPHI'S PSALM	MARY'S MAGNIFICAT
2 Nephi 4	*Luke 1*

19 Nevertheless, I know in whom I have trusted.

20 **My God** hath been my support; **he** hath led me through mine afflictions in the wilderness; and **he** hath preserved me upon the waters of the great deep.

21 **He** hath filled me with his love, even unto the consuming of my flesh.

22 **He** hath confounded mine enemies, unto the causing of them to quake before me.

23 Behold, **he** hath heard my cry by day, and **he** hath given me knowledge by visions in the night-time.

24 And by day have I waxed bold in mighty prayer before

46 And Mary said, My soul doth magnify **the Lord**,

47 And my spirit hath rejoiced in **God my Saviour.**

48 For **he** hath regarded the low estate of his handmaiden: for, behold, from henceforth all generations shall call me blessed.

49 For **he** that is mighty hath done to me great things; and holy is his name.

50 And **his** mercy is on them that fear **him** from generation to generation.

51 **He** hath shewed strength with his arm; **he** hath scattered the proud in the imagination of their hearts.

52 **He** hath put down the

(2 Nephi 4)	*(Luke 1)*
him; yea, my voice have I sent up on high; and angels came down and ministered unto me.	mighty from their seats, and exalted them of low degree.
25 And upon the wings of **his** Spirit hath my body been carried away upon exceedingly high mountains. And mine eyes have beheld great things, yea, even too great for man.	53 **He** hath filled the hungry with good things; and the rich **he** hath sent empty away.
	54 **He** hath holpen his servant Israel, in remembrance of his mercy.

We are living in a very self-centered time, a day when we are encouraged to "look within ourselves," to "find the hero within us," to "find our own truth," and so forth. We have become so focused on self-esteem, self-worth, self-expression, and self-ies that we're about to self-destruct.

You'll notice that in both Nephi's and Mary's words, there is no focus on "me, me, me" or "I, I, I." Nephi and Mary, in times of grief and in times of exultation, both look to God, the real, most reliable, and best source for appropriate feelings about ourselves. Nephi teaches us that we need not self-reliance but reliance on God when we're humbled by our own weakness. And as we display our Nativity scenes, Mary's "Magnificat" gives us just another reason to respect and admire her, not only as the mother of the Son of God but because of her magnifying God in a moment when she learned of her own special valiance and chosen status.

Christmas in a POW Camp

The idea of putting the Savior at the center of Christmas—and of our whole lives—was illustrated beautifully in an article in a Christian magazine called *Guideposts* that tells the story of a most un-usual Christmas. The story unfolds like this: Captain James Ray was a fighter pilot in the Vietnam War. He was shot down in the spring of 1966 but managed to survive. However, he was taken prisoner, and he was beaten, starved, humiliated, and forced to sign a confession.

Deprived of strength and of much of his desire to live, he said that he wished he had gone down with the plane. Finally thrown into a small, cold prison cell, he thought he heard a whisper. A fellow prisoner, speaking only when the guards were outside of hearing distance, asked him his name. This was when James Ray, whispering under his door, became acquainted with Bob Purcell, another prisoner in a nearby cell. Communicating was forbidden and punished by torture, so they were very careful, and exchanging information was a difficult and lengthy process.

In the course of their initial conversation, Bob asked James a most interesting question. He didn't ask who had won the World Series or the Super Bowl. Not anything about the stock market or the newest movie stars. Bob's whispered question from the dark, dismal prison cell was simple: "Do you know any scriptures?"

Together, with only their memories to guide them, James and Bob reassembled the Twenty-Third Psalm. You've heard it before, but read it while thinking of yourself as a prisoner, surrounded by enemies, far from home.

> *The Lord is my shepherd; I shall not want.*
> *He maketh me to lie down in green pastures: he leadeth me beside the still waters.*

He restoreth my soul: he leadeth me in the paths of righteousness for his name's sake.

Yea, though I walk through the valley of the shadow of death, I will fear no evil: for thou art with me; thy rod and thy staff they comfort me.

Thou preparest a table before me in the presence of mine enemies: thou anointest my head with oil; my cup runneth over.

Surely goodness and mercy shall follow me all the days of my life: and I will dwell in the house of the Lord for ever.

How reassuring it must have been to remember these scriptures, to recite and really believe the words "I will fear no evil: for thou art with me," even in "the presence of mine enemies."

As the war dragged on and more prisoners were taken, they were eventually moved to what was nicknamed the Hanoi Hilton. Aware of the date, some of these Christian prisoners began to plan a Christmas party. Try to imagine the scene: four men in prison pajamas, sickly and emaciated from a bad diet and numerous illnesses, began to hum, "O Little Town of Bethlehem." James reported that tears trickled through beards as they sang. Another prisoner recited—from memory—the familiar Christmas story in Luke 2: "In those days, . . . there went out a decree from Caesar Augustus, that all the world should be taxed . . ."

Suddenly someone noticed that the prison commander and some interrogators were watching, confused. They must have been feeling the spirit of Christmas, which is the Spirit of Christ, but were not aware of what it was.

That night, after months of denying repeated requests, the commander, whose heart was evidently softened a bit, brought something in to the prisoners: an English Bible. It was the first Bible they had seen since being taken prisoner. What a gift, and on Christmas Eve!

I think it's hard to imagine what life would be like without the scriptures, or what it would be like if we were forbidden to read them. These POWs opened the Bible and began to copy verses as quickly as they could. After an hour, the Bible was taken from them, and after a couple of weeks, when the spirit of the occasion was gone, the notes they had taken were also confiscated. From this experience, James Ray made an incredibly important observation:

From that we learned a most important lesson: Bible verses on paper aren't one iota as useful as Scriptures burned into your mind, where you can draw on them for guidance and comfort.

That simple observation was a Christmas gift to James and to all of us who read it today. When we get into the scriptures, eventually the scriptures get into us, and their inspired words become a power we can draw upon through thick and thin. The scriptures are not limited to just words written in books; they can become testimonies written in our hearts and can grow into a power to draw upon throughout our lives.

A Level-Three Christmas

Here we are again, my siblings and I, sitting in front of our fireplace on Christmas Eve, enjoying the anticipation of level-one Christmas.

We had no idea, in our young minds, what life had in store for us. We could not have known that one of us would have kidney problems his entire life, or that

another would spend much of her life as a single parent. We didn't know that another would not be able to have children of her own. We didn't know that another would lose a child at birth, or that yet another would suffer the pain of divorce.

We needed more than Santa Claus. A level-one Christmas wasn't going to cut it. No gift card or board game could do it. Level two wouldn't work either. We needed more than the baby Jesus. Another verse of "Away in a Manger" would be nice, but we needed more. We needed healing, not just from our sins but from the wounds we received just from living in a fallen world.

Happily, the babe of Bethlehem became the Savior, our Redeemer and our Advocate. He has been there for us, and we are grateful, because we have needed Him. We still need Him, every hour, and He is always there. He has helped us through our sicknesses, our infirmities, our pains, and our trials. Oh, how we love Him, and how we love remembering Him! The angel promised the shepherds peace on earth, and we know, by experience, where to turn for peace.

Millions of families, like mine and like yours, are taking photos this holiday season. Beautiful, innocent children are sitting beneath Christmas trees and under the stockings with very little idea what trials and triumphs lie ahead. We see the joy in their faces, and we hope they will feel the genuine joy associated with the Savior's birth.

At the same time, we ache for them—and for our own children and grandchildren—as our adult perspective informs us of what may come in their lives and in their lifetimes. But, like Nephi, we know in whom we have trusted, and, like Mary, our souls will magnify the Lord. Our testimonies of the adult Christ may be the best and most lasting gift we can leave our children so that they may know to what source they may look for the forgiveness of their sins and the healing of their hearts.

Merry Christmas to All

Like the holiday season, eventually things come to an end. But maybe Christmas itself doesn't have to have an end. Charles Dickens's closing lines in *A Christmas Carol* were about the miraculous change wrought in Ebenezer Scrooge:

> *And it was always said of him, that he knew how to keep Christmas well, if any man alive possessed the knowledge. May that be truly said of us, and all of us! And so, as Tiny Tim observed, God bless us, every one!*

To "keep Christmas well" is an intriguing thought and a worthy goal. We know we should keep the commandments, keep the faith, and keep on trying. But what does it mean to "keep Christmas"? Perhaps it means to keep remembering and practicing the lessons of Christmas every day of the year.

Christmas is a feeling. And if you're like me, it's a feeling you want to keep. May we each learn to "keep" the beautiful Christmas season at all three levels, through the day, through the season, and through a lifetime. Yes, level one is wonderful and magical, and it will carry us through Christmas Day. And level two encompasses the entire holiday season as the parties, the pageants, and the songs all look forward to the culmination on Christmas Eve. But level three, with the continuous and boundless gifts of the adult Christ, the Savior of the world, brings joy and peace that may last a lifetime.

Finally, may we keep the Spirit of Christ always as we live in joyful anticipation of future glad tidings of great joy, for the happy morning when Jesus will come again.

"The larger Christmas story is clearly not over. It is not solely about some other time, some other place, and some other people. It is still unfolding, and we are in it!"

—*Neal A. Maxwell*

NOTES

Page 3: "The spirit of Christmas illuminates . . . ," Thomas S. Monson, "The Real Joy of Christmas," 2013 Christmas Devotional. Available at churchofjesuschrist.org/broadcasts.

Page 3: "Yea, Lord, we greet thee . . . ," "Oh, Come, All Ye Faithful," *Hymns* (1985), no. 202.

Page 4: "The hopes and fears . . . ," "O Little Town of Bethlehem," *Hymns* (1985), no. 208.

Page 7: "Through all of our various Christmas traditions . . . ," Russell M. Nelson, "Christ the Savior Is Born," BYU Devotional, December 10, 2002. Available at speeches.byu.edu.

Page 9: "The Three Levels of Christmas . . . ," in William B. Smart, *Messages for a Happier Life* (1989), 33–34.

Page 17: "The joy we feel has little to do . . . ," Russell M. Nelson, "Joy and Spiritual Survival," *Ensign*, November 2016.

Page 17: "The angels and the star . . . ," Smart, *Messages for a Happier Life*, 33–34.

Page 18: "For Christmas to last all year long . . . ," Smart, *Messages for a Happier Life*, 34.

Page 21: "Love is one of the chief characteristics . . . ," Joseph Smith, *Teachings of Presidents of the Church: Joseph Smith* (2007), 426.

Page 24: "Every year, as we watch Ebenezer . . . ," L. Whitney Clayton, "Fear Not," 2015 Christmas Devotional. Available at churchof jesuschrist.org/broadcasts.

Page 31: "We could remember . . . ," Jeffrey R. Holland, "This Do in Remembrance of Me," *Ensign*, November 1995.

Page 33: "I was just beginning to learn . . . ," Kevin R. Duncan, "Heavenly Gifts," 2017 Christmas Devotional. Available at churchofjesuschrist. org/broadcasts.

Page 38: "God does notice us . . . ," Spencer W. Kimball, "Small Acts of Service," *Ensign*, December 1974.

Page 39: "Oh, how we'll make this chorus swell . . . ," "Come, Come, Ye Saints," *Hymns* (1985), no. 30.

Pages 41–42: "For Jesus, in fact, irony began . . . ," Neal A. Maxwell, "Irony: The Crust on the Bread of Adversity," *Ensign*, May 1989.

Page 45: "Is your schedule too packed? . . . ," Patrick Kearon, "Bringing Christmas into Focus," 2019 Christmas Devotional. Available at churchofjesuschrist.org/broadcasts.

Page 47: "Gift giving isn't easy . . . ," Henry B. Eyring, "Gifts of Love," BYU Devotional, December 16, 1980. Available at speeches.byu.edu.

Page 59: "At the moment of depression . . . ," Marion D. Hanks, "Make It a Good Day," address delivered at Brigham Young University, September 27, 1966. Typescript in possession of author.

Page 67: "Find someone who is having a hard time . . . ," Thomas S. Monson, "What Have I Done for Someone Today?" *Ensign*, November 2009.

Page 67: "There are chances for work . . . ," "Have I Done Any Good?" *Hymns* (1985), no. 223.

Page 68: "The same God that placed . . . ," Neal A. Maxwell, *That My Family Should Partake* (1974), 86.

Page 71: "Using one internet search engine . . . ," Joy D. Jones, "The Perfect Gift," 2019 Christmas Devotional. Available at churchof jesuschrist.org/broadcasts.

Page 80: "God lives, and his eyes are over us . . . ," John Taylor, in *Journal of Discourses*, 26 vols. (1854–1886), 23:221.

Page 82: "Brothers and sisters, can we even begin . . . ," David A. Bednar,

"The Light and the Life of the World," 2015 Christmas Devotional. Available at churchofjesuschrist.org/broadcasts.

Page 84: "The day Jesus was born . . . ," Bednar, "Light and Life."

Page 84: "Many of our memorable . . . ," Bednar, "Light and Life."

Page 87: "Jesus Christ will repair . . . ," Sharon Eubank, "Silent Night, Love's Pure Light," 2018 Christmas Devotional. Available at churchofjesuschrist.org/broadcasts.

Pages 92–94: "The woman I knew as Ann . . . ," Unpublished notes in possession of author. Used by permission.

Page 94: "Such mercy, such love . . . ," "I Stand All Amazed," *Hymns* (1985), no. 193.

Page 95: "Should we even forgive . . . ," *Teachings: Joseph Smith*, 392–93.

Page 96: "In the innocence of youth . . . ," Thomas S. Monson, "Never Alone," *Ensign*, May 1991.

Page 97: "Our Savior, Jesus Christ . . . ," First Presidency Christmas Message, 2018.

Pages 99–100: "At this time of year . . . ," Dallin H. Oaks, "Observing Christmas," BYU Management Society Address, December 9, 2015.

Page 101: "Mary's contribution to the church . . . ," Gerald N. Lund, *Jesus Christ: Key to the Plan of Salvation* (1991), 52.

Page 102: "There was only one Christ . . . ," Bruce R. McConkie, *The Mortal Messiah*, 4 vols. (1979–1981), 1:326–27 n. 4.

Page 110: "From that we learned . . . ," James E. Ray, "The Secret of Our Survival," *Guideposts*, January 1996, 10–13. Used with permission from *Guideposts*.

Page 115: "The larger Christmas story . . . ," Neal A. Maxwell, *The Christmas Scene* (2005), 11.

ABOUT THE AUTHOR

JOHN BYTHEWAY served a mission to the Philippines and later graduated from Brigham Young University. He has a master's degree in religious education and is a part-time instructor at the BYU Salt Lake Center. John is the author of many bestselling books, audio talks, and DVDs, including *How Do I Know if I Know?*; *Isaiah for Airheads*; and *Golden Answers: Why We Need the Book of Mormon*. He and his wife, Kimberly, have six children.